TENNESSEE TAILS

Pets and Their People

by

Kathryn Primm, DVM

Cover
Dr. Primm with Cheyenne
Garrett Nudd, photographer
Julie Asbill, dog owner

ISBN-13: 978-1484906149
ISBN-10: 1484906144

Dedication

This memoir is dedicated to those who love and support me—my husband, Shane; my son, Will; and my parents, who always believed in me and my dreams...

And in loving memory of Uncle Steger who made my first dream come true.

Tennessee Tails

Preface

Ask me why I love my job. Go ahead.
It's not a secret. Why do I love my job?
Because it is fun and it's worthwhile.

Why should you read this book?
Same reasons.

This chapter contains information about who
I am and how I got here. If you want to skip it
and go straight to the stories that begin on
Page 9, I don't blame you.

The fun is in the stories anyway. You can
come back and read about me later if you're
interested.

I hope these stories show you what goes
on inside my clinic, inside my head, and
inside my heart.

Enjoy!

For as long as I can remember, I dreamed of being a vet in Tennessee, which is my home. So why would a Tennessee girl go to Mississippi to study? That's easy. Mississippi State[1] offered better scholarships than did any of the other institutions that accepted me, and they had an exemplary program. When I visited, I discovered that MSU suited me well, so I "emigrated" when I finished at the Girls Preparatory School in Chattanooga.

I graduated from Mississippi State University (MSU) College of Veterinary Medicine (CVM) in 1996. Like other CVM graduates, I had a DVM[2] degree; unlike many other graduates, I was prepared for practice. MSU vets had learned sound medical and surgical skills, but more importantly, we had learned that no one can know everything.

We had been taught how to search for missing pieces and to find answers. Problem solving was something I took for granted; I assumed every professional school prepared

---

[1] One of 28 accredited programs of veterinary education in the United States.

[2] Doctor of Veterinary Medicine. Some CVMs award a VMD instead of a DVM, but it's the same degree, a prerequisite (like the Board exam we must pass) to independent veterinary practice.

students for the "real world." Having long since discovered that this is not always the case, my gratitude and my loyalty to MSU-CVM run deep.

But Tennessee is home. When it came time to establish my own practice, home to Tennessee I came. Animals and their people are special the world over, and I've had a lot of fun wherever I have found myself in seventeen years of veterinary training and practice. Because I feel a unique connection to the Volunteer State, however, my years at Applebrook Animal Hospital have been my richest yet.

All my patients and their families are memorable. Each is unique, yet all are alike, too. All our pets add joy and bring sorrow to our lives, and they will teach us if we can learn the lessons.

In this book, I am pleased to share with you the joys and sorrows, laughter and tears, and lessons it has been my privilege to experience with my patients and their people.

If you think you see your pet here, or your story (only it's about someone else's pet), perhaps you do. I have used some disguises where I thought it was appropriate, and in some cases, I may have combined characters with similar personalities or events with similar themes.

I wish I could tell all my patients' stories; I have been honored to participate in each one. This is a work of creative nonfiction, however, a collection of memoirs. I hope that you will enjoy it—that you will chuckle and choke up, get goose bumps and warm fuzzies. I hope that you will renew your appreciation for your pets and that you will understand my appreciation for all of you. I cherish you for your interest in my passion.

Tennessee Tails
Table of Contents

Applebrook Animal Hospital

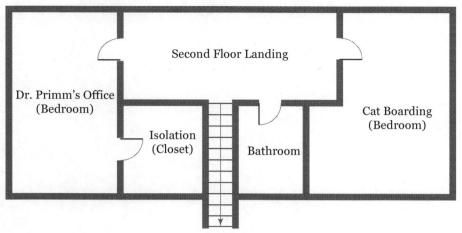

Second Floor

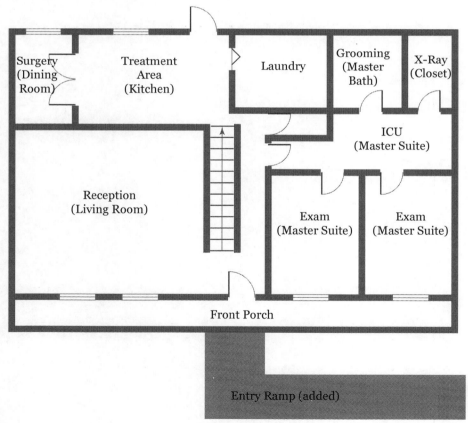

First Floor

Tennessee Tails

Introduction

If Wishes Were Horses

Veterinary practice appeals to children. They visit me regularly, but most of them outgrow their attraction to the profession as a career. I was different. I was only five when I chose my career, and I have never looked back. My husband says I'm lucky that I always knew what I wanted to do, and I couldn't agree more.

It's a daily miracle to have a worthwhile job that fits you to a T. I have that job, even though my life's course has not exactly followed my original plan, which featured a more equestrian direction.

My father has always teased that if someone had opened my head when I was little, a tiny horse would have trotted out.

Horses were always my passion: I cannot remember a time when I **didn't** love horses.

As soon as I was old enough to be my own decorator, I had horse calendars and horse posters plastering my walls and horse models decorating every flat surface in my room. I read every equine themed book in the local library and rode at every opportunity.

Most girls are afflicted with this passion sooner or later, but it's usually a passing fancy. For me, "horse crazy" was the impetus for my entire future. It started me on the road to who I am and where I am today.

We lived in the city, and despite all my pleas that a horse could surely thrive in our garage, I was able to feed my craving with live-animal contact only in the summertime, when I went to my aunt and uncle's farm.

When I was five, I asked my uncle if his farm could accommodate a horse for me to ride. He seemed skeptical, so I reassured him that he did not have to buy a new horse; I would be satisfied with a "used" one.

Shortly thereafter, Polly appeared in the paddock near his house. She was a big chestnut mare with a heart of gold.

I rode her in repetitive circles around the lot until I was so sore that I couldn't walk, but it was sheer ecstasy. Every summer after that my parents allowed me to spend several weeks at the farm with Polly.

My passion was horses, but my love has encompassed all things animal. I liked to wave at cows grazing along the road. Before I could even speak very well, I would say, "C'mere cow," to each one I saw.

Wild animals likewise enchanted me. My sisters used to wait until I was almost asleep in the car (we didn't have car seats back then, so a kid could lie down for a nap) and yell, "Look at that giraffe!" I would invariably bounce up to look, even though I knew that there was no chance I'd see a giraffe grazing along the roadside.

I would try to resist, to ignore my sisters, but they would become increasingly persuasive, describing details such as spots and eyelashes. Eventually, curiosity would get the best of me, and I would jump up again, only to hear, "Aw, you took too long. Now you've missed it!"

Animals are a gift that I have always prized.

It may be true that horses led me to veterinary school, but it was for all the animals that I stayed, and it was house pets that became my practice specialty.

Pets especially show us the meaning of unbridled joy and unconditional love. They live in the moment and relish small blessings. Their hearts are pure. If they are aggressive or difficult, there is always a reason. They are never motivated by greed or malice. They operate in survival mode entirely.

If you take the time and exercise the patience to learn who they are and how they came to be a part of the human experience, you will discover that they are with us for a reason. They make our lives better and they make us better. For each individual, that contribution is manifested very personally.

I do not treat horses anymore; my professional journey has taken a different road. Whenever my take-charge personality resists changes of plan, I remind myself of the riches that await us along life's detours.

My practice today is limited to dogs and cats, so I get the inside scoop about families' lives and relationships, giving me the matchless privilege of observing the most intimate connections between pets and their people. It is my great pleasure to share my observations with you.

1. A Mixed Metaphor

Be careful what you wish for, they say. Well, sometimes it's probably good advice. On the other hand, even the occasional nightmare can be fun.

I always wanted a Siamese kitten, exotic and beautiful, with its comical yowl and oversized personality. It was a wish deferred as I went from dorm room to pet-restricted apartment. When I finally became my own landlord, in a tiny mobile home with no roommate, everyone who knew me understood that the time had finally come for that cat.

As Christmas approached in my first year of vet school, my dear, sweet boyfriend (today my dearer, sweeter husband) longed to make my dream come true. He knew I had little time to search for fantasy kittens.

At that time in my professional evolution, my life was in the classroom, absorbing the foundations of veterinary knowledge. Classes were like run-on sentences punctuated by laboratory time. The process (whether deliberately or just as a bonus) weeds out students who lack passion and drive or maybe just grit. It claimed all our attention and all our energy.

While my mind was reeling with images of embryos at all stages of development and with diagrams of anatomical structures in various species, my boyfriend in "normal" college slipped away on a kitten hunt.

He knew he wanted a kitten that would be around weaning age at Christmas time. What he didn't know was that cats tend to stop cycling in the winter, making Christmas kittens few and far between. In rural Mississippi, Siamese kittens are darned near impossible to find at any season.

As we all know, life is about compromise...

In my darling boyfriend's single-minded determination to see me smile, he compromised "perfect seal point Siamese kitten from knowledgeable breeder" to "black farm kitten that may have some Siamese in him." (When the kindhearted farmer told Shane that the kitten's father might have been a Siamese, perhaps he was just trying to be helpful. After all, Shane did tell him he was on a desperate quest for a Siamese.)

The little creature he presented to me on Christmas Eve in a cardboard box was not exotic and beautiful, but he sure did have the Siamese yowl! He had a few other unique qualities that only made him all the more lovable to me.

He was long in body with big ears, a thick middle, and skinny legs. He was solid black with a few stray white hairs randomly scattered along his sides. You didn't notice them until he was very close, but then he appeared to be frosted.

I thought he was the most perfect kitten I had ever seen, despite (or maybe because of) his "differences."

He was not the ball of fluff that most kittens are; he looked a little like a bat. Kittens usually elicit coos and hugs; this one had a face that only a mother could love. My friends maintained a running joke that he was obviously somewhat inbred; they teased that he might be his own uncle.

Recognizing that he was my wish granted, as if by magic, I named my prize Merlin. I loved him then with all my heart and today I miss him still.

As I clawed my way through vet school, the tiny black kitten became a cat. He lay across the pages of my textbooks while I studied. He scampered across my keyboard as I worked at my computer.

The more I concentrated the more absurd his antics seemed to become. He was simply a comic delight.

He would lie in wait under my couch, peering out around the flap of fabric that hid the bottom of the couch until one of my friends or study buddies would walk down the narrow hallway to the tiny bathroom. Then he would dart out and attack their feet.

One classmate in particular, Angie, would sneak warily toward the hallway, look around anxiously, and then make a break for the potty. She would squeal in surprise every time Merlin shot out as if from a spring-loaded trap and wrapped his skinny paws around her ankles, pretending with gusto to gnaw at her leg. The room would dissolveinto giggles at her predictable dismay, and someone would have to go peel the cat peel the cat from her leg.

Merlin loved it when we laughed or shouted or did anything at all beyond our sedentary studying. He (rightfully) found vet student life quite dull and generously tried to enliven things for us at every opportunity.

When he was about 2 years old, I began the clinical portion of my training. It turned out that I never should have allowed that cat to lie on my veterinary textbooks and help me study. He obviously had learned by osmosis, because from the time I entered clinical duty, Merlin exhibited symptoms of one disease or another.

While I studied dermatology, Merlin's hair began to grow thin and fall out around his tail. It seems that when Merlin and I went to Tennessee for the summer, we had left behind some flea eggs in our mobile home. In the stifling Mississippi heat, the eggs lay in wait for our return, whereupon they hatched and set up shop on my cat's behind!

I recall bringing my stuff in from the car, hot and tired and longing for sweet tea, having to postpone my cool down when I caught sight of my white athletic socks where tiny fleas flocked like Dallas grass. Yikes!

Poor Merlin developed a hypersensitivity to flea saliva; gradually, it made his rear end bald. Strategically, he waited until I had started my dermatology rotation before he showed me this unattractive problem.

While I was learning cardiology, Merlin developed a heart murmur. I took home a stethoscope to listen to his heart from every site and from every angle.

This didn't exactly upset my attention-loving cat. Usually, I couldn't hear the murmur; frequently, not even the heartbeat was audible over the roar of Merlin's purr.

As we moved on to study the alimentary system, Merlin confronted me with chronic intermittent vomiting and diarrhea. He threw up certain foods if he ate them, and since he was not a model of dietary discretion, if he could get to them, he ate them.

One of his idiosyncrasies was pasta. Whenever I cooked spaghetti, I inevitably spilled some either from the box or as I poured it into the pot. Merlin knew the sound of falling spaghetti and would come flying from anywhere in the trailer to crunch the raw pasta with complete bliss.

Another quirk was eating (or at least chewing on) wicker furniture and cardboard of any kind; he especially relished empty toilet paper rolls or cardboard pants hangers. These items are not particularly dangerous, but would sometimes precipitate vomiting.

Intermittent vomiting was a very minor inconvenience, however, compared to his main GI problem—diarrhea. Merlin had his own room for his toys and litter box, and when his diarrhea flared up, I knew it very quickly. The worst smell **ever** emanated from his room, accompanied by a distinctive flinging sound and the pattering of the sand-like litter against his walls.

Whenever Merlin stepped in any loose stool, he would indignantly leave the litter box, glare at his contaminated foot, and shake that foot frantically until he rid it of fecal matter, sending diarrhea in all directions in a spray of foul sewage. When I heard that sound and smelled that odor, I had to dash quickly to initiate clean-up patrol because that stuff became septic concrete once it dried. Let me tell you, there is nothing like a spray of diarrhea to get a girl moving in the morning!

Having both survived my GI training, we entered my orthopedic disease rotation together. Sure enough, Merlin produced an unexplained lameness. He appeared to limp on both front feet, but then he had never seemed to run with a normal rhythm. In retrospect, I wonder if he was trying to help me learn neurology too.

You might think that these afflictions were figments of my weary imagination, but no, I wasn't hallucinating. Merlin was diagnosed officially (not by me) with flea allergy dermatitis and atopy (inhalant allergy), hypertrophic cardiomyopathy, inflammatory bowel disease, and some kind of undefined lameness. I had to provide immaculate flea control, ongoing medications for itching and heart disease, and special diet management.

Thanks to Merlin, I learned techniques that vet school doesn't cover, like how to camouflage daily meds so he wouldn't know he was getting them. Flea control was very difficult in those days before monthly flea products. However, I was strongly motivated to learn the life cycle of the flea and how to interrupt it whenever I heard my cat being called *Baboon Butt*.

Merlin made disease personal for me. I loved him. I wanted him happy and comfortable. I hoped he would live long and well. Of <u>course,</u> I studied with special concentration! Diagnosis and treatment were not just academic subjects for me, thanks to Merlin. (Do nightmares have silver linings?)

I have since had countless patients who suffered from these common feline disorders. Because of Merlin and his afflictions, I have understood their care from both sides of the examination table.

Merlin was my dream deferred, my trophy, my wish granted, my teacher, my nightmare, and my silver lining. Yes, I have seen many patients with his diseases, but I have never seen anyone besides magical Merlin who had them **all**!

2. Letting the Cats Out of the Bag

When I was still a student, surgery made me feel like a real doctor. Even today, I enter the surgery suite with a deep breath and a heartfelt prayer.

I'm a fixer: I relish the gratification and closure achieved by successful surgical repair. It also humbles me. I often wonder aloud how anyone can hold an organ and believe that life is an accident. A healthy living system is intricate and amazing, with all the parts working together for the greater good. Our ability to correct a disorder in this delicate balance is a mystery and a marvel to me.

Opening an animal's body is like entering an inner temple, one where only priests can go. When I was new to veterinary medicine, in my first job at a practice in Memphis, surgery of any kind had a mystique about it. Scrubbing in and knowing what to do made me feel as if I were privy to secret knowledge and sacred skill. To apply both for improving health excited me then and moves me still.

Reproductive control, however, makes no repair but merely alters a normal, healthy pet. Technically, it isn't much of a challenge and it lacks the suspense of reparative surgery. My goal is to get in and get out, leaving as little tissue damage as possible, and then recover the pet none the worse for the wear.

An uneventful and pain-free recovery from spaying or neutering is a source of satisfaction. The payoff in parental health and lives saved through prevention, however, is deferred and more intellectually than emotionally satisfying.

Don't misunderstand me: I'm delighted to do these procedures! They are essential to control a ballooning pet population, prolong pets' lives, and avoid needless suffering for unwanted babies. I perform them frequently, and I hope I will do many, many more.

Is it fair to say that spaying and neutering are likely to become tedious? Perhaps. Is it a mistake to take them for granted? Oh, yes.

I learned that from Callie. Her surgery taught me that there is no such thing as a "routine" operation that you can do "with your eyes closed." Her family also made a lasting impression.

I met Callie in that Memphis clinic, where we donated spaying and neutering for some shelter and rescue programs. As the last vet in the chain of command, I was designated to do these procedures to spare the other vets "all that tedium" and to continue polishing my surgical skills.

I appreciated the opportunity for learning to do a job well and knowing that I was contributing to improved quality of life for rescued animals. Nevertheless, in my arrogance, I was beginning to be bored with all these "routine" cases. Until I met Callie, that is—the outstanding exception.

She was a shorthaired, blue tortoiseshell cat, quite beautiful. She was petite, with small paws and delicate features. Her body looked too large for her tiny legs and paws, and a more seasoned or more observant veterinarian would have been alerted by this disproportion. Thanks to Callie, my pre-op examinations soon became much more meticulous!

Back then, I was focused on efficiency. I was still green, and I tended to accept the common wisdom that although this procedure was essential, it sure was monotonous.

The little cat was anesthetized and prepped according to protocol. I made my incision, beginning what I assumed was going to be a typical spaying.

As I reached in to lift up the uterus, I saw that the surgical area, called the surgical field, seemed to be overflowing with uterus. The swollen organ had three distinct lumps, each one about the size of...a newborn kitten!

I gasped and my heart skipped a beat. Suddenly, Callie had managed to gain my complete and concentrated attention.

"We have to get them out of there!" I exclaimed, galvanizing my assistants, who had begun to doze. I performed my very first C-section right there and then, with more speed and finesse than I knew I could command.

I handed each anesthetized fetus to an assistant, with instructions to rub and stimulate it. I swiftly spayed the mother so she could go on to her new home, where I sincerely hope she thrived.

I have remembered her always. I am grateful to her for teaching me to approach every surgery with my eyes, mind, and heart wide open and fully alert.

I never saw Callie again. Her offspring are the rest of the story.

Two female kittens and one male now lay on a towel in the nearby pharmacy area. As soon as I could safely scrub out, I rushed to examine my little surprises.

These three babies were very close to term: each had a full coat of hair and appeared fully developed and entirely normal. Each was opening its mouth with soundless mews, surrounded by a curious and attentive veterinary staff.

Hushed voices whispered questions and fears on two basic themes. "Is there any way they can make it?" and "What in the world is Dr. Primm going to do with these babies?"

First things first, of course. We cleaned them up and examined them. They all seemed essentially healthy, and they all said they were hungry. We placed the babies in a cardboard box with warm towels and then we raided the supply closet for baby bottles and kitten milk replacer so we could feed them.

Carrying my box of tiny felines, I returned to the office I shared with one of the senior doctors. He smiled knowingly as I hastened to explain that the kittens had surprised me in a shelter spay that morning.

I scrambled to assure him that they were not going be any problem because I had already planned for their care. That was not exactly the truth, of course, because I had NO idea what I was going to do with them. In his superior wisdom, my colleague just smiled.

"They look close to term, don't they?" I asked as we peered into box. "Do you think they can make it?"

He didn't say much except that there was only one way to find out. In that instant, I became a foster mother.

I carried those babies in my lab coat pockets during the day and took them home with me at night. I made sure they were bottle-fed every hour, on the hour. If patients or surgeries kept me from doing it myself, I called upon a ready supply of baby sitters from among my animal-loving crew.

At night, I sneaked the kittens into my tiny home. (I had nowhere near the sum required for a pet deposit. My noisy Siamese mixture, Merlin, had already been exiled to stay with my fiancé for the duration of my tenancy in this apartment.)

I rehearsed various lame excuses I hoped my landlord would fall for if he caught me harboring my little family in his no-pets-allowed apartment. I clung to the irrational hope that it would all turn out OK, reminding myself of the fact that kittens orphaned at birth can survive without nursing, unlike some animals that depend on colostrum (first milk) for their immunities.

However, baby animals get more from their mothers than nutrition. Although I was a devoted and diligent foster mom, I proved the rule that sometimes there's just no substitute for the real thing.

These kittens not only had never nursed; they had not been allowed even to remain safe in their mother until they could be born naturally. The likelihood was very strong that their lungs were underdeveloped. In addition, they had been anesthetized when we had sedated their mother.

I knew that the odds were not in favor of the tiny yellow tabbies, no matter how much I wanted or how hard I tried to save them. I also knew that little can be done for neonatal animals beyond supportive care. Their veins are too small for IVs and they are too fragile for most diagnostics.

I wish I could give you heartwarming news of incredible strength and astonishing outcomes, but this story doesn't end like that. These kittens were disadvantaged, and their ending was predictably sad. After several anxious days, they started to grow weaker one by one.

When I sought the wisdom of the senior doctors, they just shook their heads, knowing but unwilling to admit the inevitable outcome. The kittens faded away despite all my care.

I held each one close as its tiny cries grew weaker and then stopped. As the first, the second, and finally the third kitten drew its last breath, I felt more and more guilty and helpless. For a long time, I grieved their loss. I questioned my care and myself.

Did they live and die in vain? No. When I was in a strange city alone, those kittens gave me purpose. Missing Merlin, my heart was comforted by their need and their heart.

They taught me a poignant lesson that I keep learning again and again: some things I cannot fix. My job with such a patient is to **try**. If I cannot "fix it," I can rest on the knowledge that the effort made *me* better and that even if the animal could not be saved, it got the best I had to give.

Though they could not survive, those newborn kittens reaffirmed my mission, reminding me anew that it is better to have loved and lost than never to have loved at all. They confirmed why I have to be a veterinarian: I love animals, and caring for them is my calling.

3. Jackpot

When I opened my own animal hospital in 1998, my roster of patients was very small, making each patient extra special.

To this day if you showed me a list of these early patients, I could visualize and describe each one and recite details about his or her ailments, life, death, and family. I could tell you what was special to me about each one, and I remember them all very fondly.

Jake was one of those few early patients, but he would have stood out in the most crowded practice. He was a lemon pointer and a talented bird dog.

Introducing him, his owner announced, "He just works so hard for me. We are partners and I love him."

No doubt, that's why Mr. Schmidt bankrolled Jake until he hit the jackpot. You see, Jake had cancer.

Less than two months after I hung my shingle, Jake and his dad, a very tall, imposing man with a booming voice, came in for routine care. I am a small woman and I might have been intimidated by Jake's dad, but I wasn't.

His eyes twinkled above his large mustache and his palpable love for Jake encompassed me as well, because I was Jake's care provider. The three of us got along famously.

Our rapport became the starting point and foundation for a crucial 10-year partnership when an incidental finding launched us on a period of unremitting warfare.

As I examined Jake that day, I happened across a small pink bump on his glossy neck. It looked harmless enough, only about 2 cm. across. It wasn't inflamed, and touching it evoked little reaction.

I didn't feel the usual chill of dread until Mr. Schmidt told me that the tumor had appeared suddenly and seemed to be growing. Even then, I almost shrugged it off. Jake was a robust 6-year-old dog who led an active life; I saw no reason to be unduly concerned.

I certainly didn't want to alarm Mr. Schmidt unnecessarily or make a hasty decision, so I just mentioned that we should probably remove the mass for lab analysis. I described the surgical procedure that might follow if the results were positive, and I gave him a cost estimate for the whole thing.

Either the estimate must have been intimidating or I had been too reassuring, because I didn't hear back from Mr. Schmidt. After waiting with increasing uneasiness for about six weeks, I called to see if we could book the next steps for taking care of that little tumor on Jake's neck.

Mr. Schmidt was surprised to hear from me. He said the cost hadn't put him off; he just hadn't understood that the tumor was a serious problem. In my abundance of caution, I had failed to make it clear that Jake might have cancer. It need not be fatal, I replied, more firmly now, but it did need attention.

Mr. Schmidt went on to say that several other, smaller, masses had begun to appear as well, including lesions on the thigh and scrotum, which looked like the one on Jake's neck. This news intensified my concern, and I recommended more strongly that we get to the bottom of this diagnosis. We scheduled the procedures for the following week.

All the pre-anesthetic testing was normal, showing that Jake was healthy and strong enough for the operation. We proceeded with the mass removal and histopathology (submitting the tumors to the lab for sectioning and review). At Mr. Schmidt's request, I removed only the two largest masses, waiting to see if the lab results warranted more aggressive surgery.

During the surgery, I did an impression smear, a preliminary inspection performed by pressing the inside of the mass against a glass microscope slide and then staining it. I was shocked to see cells that appeared malignant. They looked like a population of mast cells, not at all what I had expected or ever wanted to see.

Mast cell tumors are rather common in dogs, and they don't always mean a death sentence, but they are malignant, carrying the threat of metastasis and other serious consequences. This type of tumor requires an aggressive surgical margin (removal of more tissue surrounding the tumor on all sides). That meant Jake needed a somewhat more invasive resection than if the preliminary cytology had not been so worrisome.

A few days later, the histopathology report confirmed my suspicions. A few weeks later, Jake's dad called reporting more tiny masses that looked like the first ones. He was concerned enough to just book the surgery this time without any further examination. He didn't even ask for a cost estimate.

No wonder he was anxious! I found nine more masses on Jake's scrotum and thighs. Aggressive resection would be impossible without removing the scrotum and testicles. Since I knew that Jake was a hunting dog and Mr. Schmidt might be reluctant to have him neutered, I called to suggest a referral for radiation therapy.

Mr. Schmidt promptly informed me that Jake was much more important than hunting. If they never hunted again, he stated emphatically, it didn't matter; he just wanted to keep Jake with him. He instructed me unequivocally to go ahead and perform the recommended procedure.

Everything went well, and Jake recovered from the anesthesia and operation without incident. They went home with post-op instructions that included daily inspections to detect any new masses.

Paying close attention is critical to a favorable outcome because mast cell tumors are less likely to metastasize if they are removed while they are still small. I knew by now that I could trust Mr. Schmidt to be a faithful observer. He would notify me as soon as any new problems developed.

Almost a whole year went by before I next saw Jake, when his routine wellness visit coincided with the return of his tumors. One of the masses that I had removed from his neck had returned, and there was a new one on one of his ears.

I recommended another removal. We had experience now; we knew that Jake recovered easily and could be expected to suffer no ill effects from the cancer or the surgery. Mr. Schmidt readily agreed; we were again favored with an uneventful surgery.

Before I discharged Jake, I showed Mr. Schmidt where the lymph nodes for that region reside, cautioning him even more strongly than before to monitor Jake for other signs of metastasis. This recurrence on Jake's neck was in an especially bad place, where metastasis would be both much likelier and much more dangerous.

It seems that when a cancer recurs at the site of a previous surgical excision, it comes back with a vengeance. Many of these returning masses behave more aggressively, and I was starting to worry now.

Sure enough, Jake was back early the next year with enlarged cervical lymph nodes on the right. An aspirate confirmed my fear that it was a mast cell invasion of the lymph tissue, from where it could be expected to spread rapidly throughout the system.

Trying not to convey my sense of helplessness and dismay, I spoke candidly with his owner. Lymph node involvement upped Jake's cancer scale and changed his prognosis for the worse. Surgical removal wasn't as promising a treatment option this time, and again I offered referral.

Mr. Schmidt was unwavering. He still wasn't willing to subject Jake to the more aggressive radiology or chemotherapy treatments and he refused my referral to the oncology center. He wanted me to just de-bulk the tumor that was hindering Jake's breathing and eating.

Grimly, I set to work on the tumor, doing my best to remove every last ounce of that tissue. My confidence was at low ebb. Without ancillary treatment, I had to give this lovely, valiant dog a fair-to-poor prognosis, gambling on a survival of maybe 3 months.

During the next year, I saw Jake every few months, each time performing several additional mass removals. Jake had a terrific attitude about his medical care: he never seemed to object to being handled or undergoing treatment.

Every time they returned, he eagerly dragged his owner into my hospital and greeted me with a wag. He seemed to know that we were helping him and that we had seen him safely (somehow) through three years of cancer. As long as the casino was open, he was coming to play.

We continued to roll the dice, and eventually, the mass in Jake's lymph nodes was gone. It never returned, and no new tumors appeared. I was amazed and grateful, exhilarated that I had been so wrong!

I had first seen Jake in 1998 and now it was 2003. Here he was five years later, completely happy. He was even hunting! Mr. Schmidt laughingly referred to Jake as my "cash cow," and indeed the costs of his care had been nontrivial.

It seemed to me like a high-stakes gamble that had paid off. Each costly surgery was done with love and prayer, and the hope that it would be the last one. Amazingly, it finally was—WE HAD A WINNER!

I saw Jake every year after that for his wellness visit, but he rarely needed me for anything else, as he remained healthy and fit. After his last surgery in 2003, Jake lived another five years; when he left us in 2008, he was a respectable 16 years old.

I still see Mr. Schmidt occasionally, when he comes in with his son and his son's dog, but he obviously has never found another dog for himself. He says his heart was broken when he finally lost Jake, and he could never love another dog. I understand. Theirs was a special bond strengthened by trials repeated and optimism rewarded.

Cancer is a weighty diagnosis for anyone, and medical advancements for animals don't always keep pace with those for human patients, so the prognosis for animals may be much poorer.

In Jake's case, however, that didn't even matter, because his dad didn't want to subject him to heroic measures anyway. All we did was excise those tumors every time they returned, until finally, miraculously, we had the last move.

I will always remember Jake's bravery, his resilience, and that unfailingly merry attitude. Was that what made the difference? Was it Mr. Schmidt's devoted persistence, not counting the cost? Or did their special friendship work magic in the same way as kissing the dice?

4. Faith under Pressure

My hospital building was a residence when I acquired it. Making it into a functional hospital (see sketch of floor plan at p. xvii) took considerable modification, and the construction materials included the blood, sweat, toil, and tears that my family and I invested in the process.

The renovation was a challenge to my budget, and Mr. Schmidt isn't entirely wrong to suppose that Jake helped me retire that loan. With only my parents as clients when I opened my doors, and very few others for some time thereafter, I had more time than money in the early months.

To make ends meet, we patched, spackled, and painted. We hired contractors for only the biggest projects, tasks we just couldn't handle by ourselves. The building is filled with indelible memories of hard fun and playful labor.

As we toiled, I imagined with excitement what the empty rooms would be like in the buzz of a busy workday. The transformation from former residence to future hospital was a labor of love and hope.

As the years have gone by and those hopes have been realized, ever more love has been absorbed into the hospital's walls. I recall with undiminished emotion the day Faith came to me, bringing love, along with courage, hope, and great fear.

On that memorable day, I saw my allergist striding purposefully up the handicapped-accessible ramp that enters Applebrook Animal Hospital. Through the windows of the master bedroom that became my examining rooms, I can see the street and that ramp, often getting a hint of what's coming our way.

The special manner in which someone carries an animal in trouble—or simply carrying an animal that would not ordinarily be carried—warns of emergency. Sometimes the alarm is conveyed by the sense of urgency or fear on a person's face.

Other times, I am notified in advance that there is an emergent situation, and I watch for the patient's arrival so I can begin my preliminary assessment of its need.

With non-verbal patients, I depend on subtle clues like stiffness of gait or muscular tension, or not-so-subtle signs like loss of consciousness. It stands to reason that I want to know from such signs as much as I possibly can even before the door opens.

On what I think of as the day of the revival, Dr. Berrie carried his family's 70-pound German Shepherd into the house's former living room, now my hospital's reception area. It was a spring evening and things had begun to slow down for the day.

In the spring, as the days grow longer, our business becomes feast or famine. Fewer clients want to schedule routine care: in the grip of spring fever, sensible persons prefer to be out on bikes or enjoying the nearby mountains. More of our clients at this season are seeking care that can't be postponed. Once the freshness of spring starts to subside, routine visits pick up, but spring is notorious for sick pets and emergencies.

Calculating the statistics for spring emergency visits, factoring in the time of day, and observing the mode of Faith's arrival, I felt the frisson that signals my brain to put its affairs in order stat. I could tell that this big dog was in big trouble, and I summoned one of my assistants immediately.

Watching her dad, a doctor trained not to panic, hustling up the ramp with Faith in his arms, we knew that we were facing a crisis. I could not have predicted what kind.

Faith was a beautiful pup, only 8 months old, whom I had seen once before. On this memorable visit, my assistant ushered a surprisingly calm Faith and her surprisingly apprehensive owner straight to the treatment room at the back of the hospital (formerly the kitchen) where Dr. Berrie told us this all-too-exciting tale.

His school-age sons had been playing in tall grass near their home, stretched out full-length on the ground, hiding from each other. Faith was with them, reveling in their noisy companionship, as puppies do.

Suddenly, the boys had told him, she had stopped playing and become agitated, whining and wriggling frantically. Since they had no idea what she was up to, they ignored her and resumed their play, but Faith continued to act weird, they said.

Finally, when she could see that they weren't going to pay attention—and who knows what else may have happened that they couldn't see—she just sat down...right on the snake about which she'd been trying so desperately to warn them.

When Faith yelped in pain but did not move, the boys realized she must be in danger. They checked it out and finally understood her warning when they saw the snake she had caught under her haunch.

At that, they raced to tell their father what had happened. (As if he weren't already sufficiently horrified, one of them thought to add that the snake looked like a copperhead. Might that explain why this man who is *always* calm was a little less so this evening?)

As soon as the boys started running toward home, Faith decided it was safe to leave her post, and she followed them, holding up her right rear leg.

Within 15 minutes, Dr. Berrie was at my office with Faith, and I was clipping her hair over the stifle. I saw two blackened puncture wounds, leaking fluid that ran slowly down her leg like toxic ooze. Her pale gums, rapid heartbeat, and elevated respiratory rate told me she was in a state of shock that called for emergency medical management.

I hastily placed an intravenous catheter that would allow emergency access to Faith's vein as well as providing a port to administer lifesaving fluids and drugs. Then we hooked up the EKG that would permit us to monitor her heart.

What we still needed was antivenin. Like a vaccine made from the serum of an animal infected by the disease the vaccine will prevent, antivenin is made from the serum of an animal that has developed immunity to snake venom. It is not a preventative, of course, as a vaccine is, but it can usually forestall the worst consequences of snakebite.

Antivenin is technically difficult to manufacture and therefore very expensive. General practices and pharmacies seldom have the injection on hand. When I called the local animal trauma center, therefore, I wasn't surprised to learn that they had no antivenin.

As two doctors must, Dr. Berrie and I faced the facts. Without antivenin, Faith's snakebite must be very painful, and we had to consider that it could be life threatening.

In my experience, the worst snakebites in animals are those closest to the throat, where they cause airway constriction. Faith's injury, thankfully, was on her rear leg because she had sat on the snake. She was not facing imminent death, perhaps, but she was still at risk and she was suffering.

Realizing gratefully that Faith had sustained the attack protecting his children, Dr. Berrie wanted to do everything possible to spare her any pain we could and to prevent even the slightest risk of death.

Suddenly an idea came to me.

Antivenin works the same whether the snake's victim is an animal or a person, but an animal's necessary dose is infinitesimal compared to the dose a human requires. If I had no more than a single vial, it would be enough to make a difference for Faith.

All I had to do was locate that one vial.

Dr. Berrie and I shared and still share a medical respect for each other and have always been able to speak candidly as colleagues. He had helped me save my career earlier that year when he had diagnosed me with animal allergies, of all things!

Utterly unprepared for that diagnosis, I had been unable to disguise my unbidden tears as I imagined my life without animals.

"Do I have to sell my horses and quit my job?" I implored. Dr. Berrie had calmly supported me through my meltdown.

"You are my vet," he had said firmly. "Quitting is NOT an option!" He assured me that together we would find a way to manage, and he was as good as his word.

He had treated me so effectively that I had kept my job and my pets. He had saved my life, or at least what gave it much of its meaning. With all my heart, I wanted to come through for him and Faith now that they were depending on my expertise. With just a little anitvenin, I could do it.

I called the local trauma center for humans and spoke to an animal-loving pharmacist. Hearing the story of Faith's heroism, he recognized the importance of what I was asking of him.

He had antivenin he could give me, he said, but he couldn't entrust it to just anyone. Since I couldn't leave Faith and my staff couldn't leave the hospital, that left only Dr. Berrie to pick up the medication. You can imagine our rejoicing when the pharmacist agreed to release a single vial of the antivenin to Dr. Berrie for me to use on the Berries' dog.

That was a long night. My loyal staff all stayed long past closing to help as we cared for Faith, treating her shock and her symptoms, while Dr. Berrie rushed downtown to the trauma center for the antivenin. As soon as he returned, we started the slow process of dripping the medicine through Faith's IV.

Bags and keys forgotten by the door, we fetched chairs from around the hospital and pulled them up close to the table where she lay. The silence of apprehension draped the room like a fog. No one wanted to leave. We were tied there, waiting for the outcome and praying for a happy ending.

Because antivenin is recognized as a foreign substance by the patient's immune system, it must be administered under very close supervision so that allergic reactions can be reversed before they escalate beyond control. We all watched Faith as if she were a pot that wouldn't boil, checking her vitals and assuring that all was as it should be. I racked my brain for anything else we could do to help...antihistamines, pain coverage, constant companionship.

Our prayers were answered; Faith developed no untoward reactions during any part of her treatment. I had given her analgesics and antibiotics to protect her damaged tissues, prevent complications, and ease her recovery, and she responded so well that once the antivenin was on board and she seemed to stabilize, I was willing to allow her to recover at home with her family.

I had a feeling no one at the Berrie house had much peace until we called to report that she was out of the woods. I knew they wanted her home, and I knew I could trust them to take especially good care of her!

Within two days, she was bearing weight on the leg, despite some remaining swelling. The bruising resolved and Faith was treated like a queen at home.

She preferred to behave like a playmate, of course, even after she had long outgrown her puppy days. Faith proved her resilience and lived a long and happy life. She confronted hip dysplasia and osteoarthritis as an old dog, but her family always treated her with tenderness. They never forgot what they owed her for her first act of love and self-sacrifice, when she had showed more than an ordinary puppy's maturity, forethought, and devotion.

When the Berrie family's Faith was endangered, together we provided protection, though it was a close call. Their relationship to Faith was never the same and the walls of my clinic were enriched by another layer of love, courage, and triumph.

The snake was never heard from again.

5. Peace through Strength

The Roman emperor Hadrian built his wall across Britain to secure peace through strength. Butch would have understood that, although he did not deal in walls, and his was not military strength but strength of character.

Butch was an older cat, a portly domestic short hair, white with black spots. He was chatty and sociable. When he was in the clinic, I could recognize his voice as soon as I came through the door.

I looked forward to the days when he stayed with us; he seemed grateful for our care, and he returned the love we gave him many times over. Butch was our guest quite frequently, because he suffered from diabetes, a chronic disease that is common in companion pets.

Diabetes management demands vigilant care, requiring high levels of attention and commitment. It involves lots of needle sticks,not just to administer insulin but to monitor blood glucose, first to define the disease and then to monitor insulin response.

Human patients understand the endless monitoring and the perpetual needles as animals cannot. Among pets with diabetes, it is only their faith in humans that sustains their spirits and their cooperation.

Butch was a pliable patient. He would gently knead the air with his feet while I drew his blood again and again. He would rub on his cage door in anticipation of being released, even though he knew that getting out would likely be followed by blood tests. He didn't care. The attention was worth the irritation of restraint and needles.

This cat never once struggled or responded with aggression or even showed annoyance during any of the endless series of diagnostics and medications I ordered. He was mellow and pleasant in the face of adversity. He erected no defenses. He exemplified a life well lived.

Time marches forward and medicine advances, but at that time, diabetes care at Applebrook included frequent inpatient stays with hourly blood samples. We tweaked our treatment plans and watched him closely, and something we did for Butch worked. He lived for years with his diabetes, and his quality of life was wonderful.

Not only did Butch enrich my days with his placid optimism, but so also did his owner, Gwen (who is still a dearly loved client). Gwen herself has battled disease; she is a breast cancer survivor. I like to think that walking her path with Butch helped her build the sunny resilience with which she carried on.

When her dark hair fell out, she seemed grateful just to be alive. When I knew that she felt the opposite of strong, she wore the same smile that has always lighted her face.

An owner who listens and asks good questions, I imagine that she brought to her own care the same intelligence and determination she applied to Butch's care.

Gwen makes my job easy and her pets happy. Caring for Butch, she followed my instructions as closely as possible.

She patiently administered daily injections. She watched food intake and diet. She kept up with the smallest details of his daily status, so we could detect the slightest changes for better or worse.

Gwen loved and appreciated Butch for how much he added to her life. Caring for him in his illness was a responsibility and a debt that she gladly paid.

Because of the extraordinary combination of conscientious owner and compliant patient, Butch responded and flourished despite his chronic diabetes.

In fact, it wasn't diabetes that killed him; he died of old age. He suffered other organ failures as he grew old, and eventually a tough decision had to be made.

As any pet owner knows, the relative life span of pets compared to humans is one of nature's meanest tricks, against which there is no appeal. Euthanasia is always difficult and I do my best to support owners facing this excruciating decision.

Love is very hard when it means letting another creature go, especially when the end of its pain is going to hurt you more than you even want to contemplate. Families bring to the decision their own issues with death and relationships, and I try to be sensitive to each situation.

It helps that I know my clients, having gone with them through such a variety of incidents with their pets. I can reminisce with them about funny antics, bullets dodged, or stories they have shared over the years. Medically, I can also acknowledge the suffering, the cost of heroic measures, and the poor odds of survival for a very sick animal and validate the family's investment of love and support.

When a much-loved animal has reached his time to leave, there is no easy way to separate. Some families can't bear to be present for the event. Others feel like they have to be there, no matter how wrenching, to see their pet off on his last adventure. Gwen chose to remember Butch as he had been at home, in his happiest places, so she remained in our waiting room with her thoughts.

The vet has no choice in the matter. My job is to be there, to officiate at this ceremony with dignity and respect that honor the needs of the pet and the owner. I find that being present is very powerful.

I was touched when Gwen let Butch go with us, responsive to our need to say goodbye to him here at the hospital where he had been such a delightful fixture. I was proud that she entrusted him to us, knowing he loved us and would feel safe with me at the end.

I held him close as I humanely gave him his final injection. Memories caved in on me. I could hear his joyful greetings. I could see his black and white paws gently kneading the air one last time.

All went as expected, and he was at peace. I wrapped him in a blanket and carried him back to his owner.

I am a communicative person but as I handed Butch back to Gwen, I could find no words. A sob rendered me silent and tears filled my eyes. I felt a hole in my heart where Butch had lived.

I thrust Butch into Gwen's arms and hurried from the room just ahead of hysterics. Every part of me felt awful.

I had not been a pillar of strength for Gwen, who had been so strong for Butch. Yes, I had been there for Butch, but I felt I had fallen far short of my responsibility to his beloved owner.

I wrote Gwen a heartfelt note of condolence for Butch's loss and apology for failing her at a critical moment. She replied with great kindness, erasing my shame by saying she was glad that I had loved him too and that my grief had meant more to her than all the pillars of strength ever could.

I know she is comforted, as I am, to think of Butch waiting for her across Rainbow Bridge, diabetes-free. He was my patient, but we had more than the usual vet-patient relationship because he was with me so much and he was such a darling. I loved and cared for him as if he were my own. He rewarded me in full.

When friends later teased me about my breakdown, saying, "What? You mean you are human?" I was not amused. Butch taught me to be both a better human being and a better professional caregiver.

He saw the bright side in everything. He obviously thought, "Well, here we go. She is going to stick me with a needle again, but she will hold me and pet me and I know it will be worth it."

If you can see the bright side of spending another day at the hospital...

If you can greet your medical providers each time with a joyous hello...

If you can think of the pain they inflict as loving care...

If you can relish unappetizing food...

If a gentle pat on the head can always make you ecstatic...

Then you can be as inspiring as Butch was.

You will be content, others will rally to support you, and you too can know peace through strength.

6. Baby Daddy

Puppies don't care about their lineage. If they are loved and cared for, then they will be loyal and affectionate.

Puppies are wiggling, wagging, grinning bundles of happiness. My staff and I adore puppy visits. The puppy room is always filled with love, joy, and a sense of potential.

Hopes and dreams ride on those little canine backs. No matter what the size of a pup, he or she carries those hopes and dreams with pride and enthusiasm.

You cannot be gloomy around an energetic puppy filled with the zest of life. I defy anyone to watch a puppy's initial clinic visit without breaking a smile.

On the first workday of the New Year, old and new clients were trickling in with Christmas puppies. As I slipped into the exam room, a tan blob, mostly feet and ears, tumbled clumsily between my ankles.

He was unusually endearing, with soulful eyes and pleading posture. He was quiet at that moment, but I was thinking that he probably barked as if he were on the scent with a mounted horseman.

His coat was glossy and short, a golden tan. He had low-set floppy ears and a round little head. His face was already a testament to the force of gravity.

His owner was a tall man with sandy blonde hair, a calm manner, and an air of kindness—a southern gentleman named Tom, who I knew had met with great sorrow. I could see that today, to life's rollercoaster of agony and ecstasy, this pup was bringing nothing but pure happiness.

I had met Tom before with other pets, but as this puppy bounded to meet me, I could tell he was something special. His man was beaming with pride.

I made all my usual new puppy inquiries about appetite and housebreaking, and Tom answered each one in a warm Southern drawl. Then, as I always do at the end of a visit, I asked if he had any questions.

I was ready for, "So, doc, any idea what kind of dog he is?"

I had already ticked off the possibilities in my head.... Coonhound? Walker hound? Blue Tick? I would even entertain the possibility of Bloodhound. Certainly, my best guess was that it was going to have "hound" in it.

You can imagine my surprise when Tom asked, "So doc, when is Boomer's hair gonna get all long and curly?"

I paused, not quite sure where he was going with this question.

"Long and curly?" I queried, stalling.

"Yeah, he's a Golden Retriever. There were 11 of 'em and they all looked just alike."

I thought for a moment, not wanting to dim the blissful aura in the puppy sanctum. He gazed at me in suspense, patiently waiting for my answer.

Images of his hopes and dreams flashed through my head. Playing ball with a leaping retriever and swimming at the lake sprang to mind. How I wanted that for him. OK, I thought to myself, tread softly.

Turning my best smile on him, I replied, "Would you believe never?"

Taken aback, he slumped in his chair, silently digesting this new information. I hastily explained that Golden Retriever pups were born with longer hair than Boomer would ever see and that he was a wonderful puppy, no matter his lineage.

"I saw his mother," Tom said in some confusion. "And his father...they were beautiful Golden Retrievers."

I asked him if he had seen how the dogs were penned. He explained that both parents were in a fenced back yard. No other dogs were allowed entry into their yard.

"Chain link fence, you say? The kind with the big holes in it?"

He nodded.

"And with those swinging gates that come unlatched fairly easily when largish dogs leap against them?"

Again, he nodded, more slowly this time, comprehension beginning to dawn.

I went on somewhat tentatively to show him the traits that I recognized as hound characteristics. He had come in so full of pride in his new puppy. I did not want to diminish his delight, to see him return this precious puppy or to become frustrated in his sudden disappointment.

He drew in a deliberate breath and said, "He's registered! I sent in the papers. What do I do now?"

Routine DNA testing on purebred dogs had not begun yet, so I asked him if he was planning to breed Boomer.

Tom explained that Boomer was to be a companion and pet; in fact, he already had planned to have him neutered. He saw my trepidation and smiled.

"I love him anyway, don't worry. He's my good friend."

A friend he remained. He walked with his owner through sickness and health, offering his comfort to a bereaved heart. He needed Tom and diverted him. He provided companionship and amusement. They loved each other.

I diagnosed Boomer with lymphoma some years ago and Tom opted for chemotherapy.

Animals do very well with such treatment, and Boomer was no exception. His cancer stayed in remission for a long time.

His quality of life was excellent; he didn't even know he'd ever had cancer. He brightened Tom's days with his steadfast presence as long as he lived.

Tom told me once that before Boomer, he had lost his wife and unborn child in an accident, and it had changed him forever. He knew of love and loss. He stood by Boomer the way Boomer stood by him and he valued his unfailing love, maybe more than anyone else could have.

Only Boomer's mama knew for sure who his daddy was. But we all knew what kind of dog Boomer was...

Boomer was a godsend.

7. A Cat in the Hand

Kentucky was a unique cat, well worth two in the kennel, and I miss him still. It's true that every cat is an individual, but Kentucky was in a class by himself.

He was a big yellow tabby, but not the usual yellow. He was almost peach colored, stout, with short hair and extraordinarily large green-yellow eyes. Kentucky's family traveled frequently, and he spent a lot of time boarding with us.

In my original renovation of the house, I had converted an upstairs bedroom to a "cat room," away from barking dogs and the hubbub of daily work at my small animal practice. The cat room was next to my office, so I would wander in frequently to pet the cats between patients. (OK, or when I ought to have been performing administrative duties—but seriously, aren't cats more fun than stale piles of paperwork?)

Kentucky craved attention and soon discovered that he could sucker **me** specifically into responding to his call. When I arrived on the mornings when he was in residence, his yowls resounded through the entire hospital, beginning at the first moment the sound of my voice reached his ears. If I replied from a distance, he only intensified his calls. He wanted me to be *right there*

.He was my funny, friendly, "Welcome-back-What-took-you-so-long-I-am-so-happy-you-are-here" guy, and no one ever made me feel more important. Our relationship made my day on so many mornings, but like many relationships, this one had a teeny, tiny, little shadow that doomed it. Kentucky was funny and friendly only to humans.

He had a deep-seated hatred of all other cats. When he so much as glimpsed another cat, a growl would well up from the very heart of him that threatened severe bodily harm to someone unless the other cat vanished posthaste or sooner.

Being the obedient servants we were, we strove to keep Kentucky's line of sight strictly cat-free. We rigged up curtains. We turned, slanted, and tilted cage banks. We juggled the boarding calendar. It became second nature for us to manipulate Kentucky's environment to his liking, and we didn't give it much thought any more.

Until that fateful day when Kentucky's family arrived to retrieve him...

His #1 most well trained servant, I went up to get him. Fetching patients is not usually my job; I am usually too busy with other things. On this day, to my everlasting regret, I went to get Kentucky myself so I could tell him goodbye.

Although I'm not very involved with our healthy boarders (with notable exceptions like Kentucky), I do usually expect to know who is in our care. On this particular day, however, a quiet wallflower cat had arrived while I was at lunch. Jenny, our new receptionist, not yet experienced in "Kentucky management," had checked in this new cat without calling his presence to my attention.

Focusing on Kentucky, I failed to notice the iron-grey cat crouched in the stainless steel cage across from his. Kentucky hadn't noticed it either...until... Holding him in my arms as if he were a baby, I turned to pick up his bag of treats and belongings.

Oops. My turn brought Kentucky face to face with the alien cat when I leaned over for the bag. The demon entered into Kentucky's soul with a low growl that vibrated my hand.

I still didn't notice the other cat. I didn't pause in my movement toward the alien beast until Kentucky catapulted himself toward its cage. With his bag in my right hand, I reflexively reached for Kentucky with my left.

Suddenly sure that he was in the clutches of the invader, Kentucky clamped down hard on the hand restraining him—mine. With a strength and ferocity that only the conviction of imminent death could have provoked, he sank his little teeth deep into my flesh and held on for dear life.

Paralyzed now beyond fight or flight, at least Kentucky had the presence of mind to recognize me. He somehow managed to hold still while I dropped the bag from my right hand and pried his teeth from my left. He was still terrified, though; his pupils were widely dilated as I placed him in his carrier.

In my concern for Kentucky's fright, my pain did not register, but having treated more cat bites than I can count, I knew exactly how bad they could be. My hand was fast approaching that condition.

The injury was deep and already swelling as I called my husband. Employed in human medicine and not lacking good sense, he sorted out my priorities and sent me straight to a hand surgeon he knew. On my behalf, he even called the surgeon, who agreed to meet me at the hospital right away.

I was at the ER within the hour. One of my clients, Jayna, efficiently checked me in, admirably concealing her confusion at this role reversal. She was shocked and alarmed to learn that I was there for treatment of a cat bite, and she made my expedition through triage as quick and easy as possible. I can't thank her enough for lending me her expertise and moral support.

After the doctor had taken a quick look, he asked, "When was the last time you ate?" I knew I was headed for surgery.

Too bad for them, I was stuffed with lasagna, and the surgeon had to mend my injured hand using only local anesthesia, with me awake to seek information and demand explanations. Oh, the poor guy!

Worst of all, the dissociative medications he gave me rendered me unusually talkative. I queried him at every step of the way, in the interest of comparing human versus animal medical practice, apparently.

Luckily for both of us, the surgeon had a sense of humor as well as a great deal of skill. He somehow accomplished very good work on my hand while maintaining what I believed was rational conversation. (I heard that he later described me as "interesting.") What a nice guy!

Kentucky's tooth had penetrated the tendon sheath of my ring finger. Following surgery, a splint immobilized my hand for several weeks, and the wound became infected despite its prompt treatment.

After working one-handed for several weeks and following tiresome medical orders to the letter, I was elated when my hand became fully functional again. With only a tiny scar on my palm and no residual scar at all on the back of my hand, the only lasting effect is a slightly weakened grip. Sometimes now, I have to get help opening a jar.

My grip would have weakened anyway in 20-30 years, and even losing the use of my hand for a little while was nothing in the larger scheme of things. The worst of it was that I lost my darling Kentucky.

Although I still cared for other cats in his family, his owner wouldn't bring Kentucky back to me. She told me that she would find another vet for him to bite.

I tried to explain to her that it was my fault for lack of vigilance, but she would not relent. Although it was only an accident—Kentucky was just being himself, as he had always warned he would—she has not forgiven his lapse in manners.

Maybe someday she will be able to see it my way and to give credit to the part of him that recognized me and came back from adrenaline frenzy before he bit clean through my hand.

Many cats still board with us, and I wish that Kentucky were among them—demanding, finicky, peculiar, fierce, and dependent—

giving me another chance to be uniquely important to an irreplaceable friend.

8. Out of the Closet

If any animal (besides Kentucky) should be isolated from others, it's an animal affected with parvoviral enteritis, a completely disgusting and extraordinarily contagious disease. It is characterized by vomiting, lethargy, and profuse bloody diarrhea, which is associated with a distinctive, unpleasant odor. The infected dog will become depressed (wouldn't you?) and die in the absence of effective treatment.

I don't see parvovirus here very often because it is easily prevented today by routine vaccination, but some places still have it in epidemic proportions. The occasional cases that occur are in puppies that have not been vaccinated or have been incorrectly vaccinated by breeders or owners who lack appropriate training.

When I first opened Applebrook, before widespread community education about appropriate vaccination, I did see several cases of dogs sick with the dreadful parvovirus. Reinforcing my education and training, that direct experience turned me into a relentless campaigner for vaccination.

I am frightened and frustrated when I encounter the attitude that vaccination is no longer important now that the disease has been brought under control. Parvovirus has not been eradicated. If we stop vaccinating, it will come roaring back because there are still areas where it is endemic, where all puppies are exposed, and too many are still affected by the disease.

These heart-wrenching cases are usually in puppies around 5-6 months of age, just starting to lose their neonatal immunities, with their own immune systems not quite ready to protect them. If a puppy's immune system is still naïve to the parvovirus and not supported by vaccination, the puppy gets very sick, very quickly, which is the story of Darla and Duffy.

When we renovated what became Applebrook Animal Hospital, a "luxury" we couldn't afford and therefore had to defer was an isolation facility. Parvovirus, however, is so extremely contagious that quaranting affected animals is not negotiable and can never be compromised.

When the early parvovirus cases started to creep in, therefore, I had to make some accommodation for their isolation. In my new facility, the only nook that was not in a traffic lane was my office upstairs. A former bedroom, it still had a walk-in closet. Here we outfitted a makeshift isolation ward with portable kennel cages and IV equipment. We even rigged up a footbath, filling a cat litter box with antiseptic so that we could disinfect our shoes before leaving the "isolation ward."

On the day Darla and Duffy arrived, very sick with parvovirus, I suited myself up like an astronaut in a hazmat suit and carried them resolutely up to my office.

These two new puppies were darling tricolor Bassett hounds, with the breed's distinctive droopy eyes and ears bigger than my whole hand. They also had what I have come to think of as "The Look."

A parvo patient has an unmistakable expression not defined by medical science. It is something I have learned to recognize from experience, a pathetic look of defeat pleading for help as they gaze up at you. More than the typical Basset sad face, these parvo victims had The Look.

I call them victims because they had been home vaccinated by their breeder. Obviously, without training in immunology, breeders are less likely to find, choose, and purchase effective vaccines and to administer them often enough at medically appropriate intervals under ideal conditions.

New owners naturally, albeit unwisely, accept breeders' assurances that their puppies have "had everything" necessary to grow and thrive for the next year. Innocent puppies pay the price. I always encourage new owners to bring breeders' records to me for review as soon as possible to make sure puppies do in fact get "everything." For these poor babies, that hadn't happened.

Frontline providers had failed to deter the enemy parvo, and now I would be taking the last shot. As I engaged in battle against the effects of the disease in those puppies, I could only hope that my weapons were not too few, too weak, or too late.

As we mounted our defense, I was satisfied with our resourcefulness and our success at ensuring isolation and hygienic procedure. I was satisfied, that is, until diarrhea took over.

With it came The Odor, unlike anything else in the olfactory repertoire. It is indescribably repugnant—the smell of death, which left untreated, is exactly what it is going to become.

Having valiantly sacrificed my closet for medical necessity, we began aggressive fluid replacement therapy and other treatments that might help the puppies fight the parvoviral enteritis. As the disease progresses, the odds of beating it grow ever smaller, and Darla and Duffy were already dehydrated and well into the disease before I saw them.

Nevertheless, we refused to be dismayed. I gave the pups a 50/50 chance of recovery and took up watch in my office, peering into the closet frequently. Since we had just opened, we were not too busy for me personally to keep vigil over these sick pups, gently attending to their every need.

I could envision a green vapor emanating from that closet, the kind of miasma you see on Looney Tunes, but that terrible smell did not deter me. Those puppies needed my help and they were going to get it.

I checked IV fluids and gave injections. I cleaned up foul diarrhea every few minutes and cleaned the puppies too as best I could. I made sure that they were warm and as comfortable as I could make them, and I ensured that they never felt alone.

I promised them that if they could just hang on, I would do everything I could to support them while their bodies fought the fight. (Anyone who has cared for the sick knows that you talk to them and confide in them, coaxing them to get well, holding onto their spirits with your voice.)

Despite my best efforts, my 50/50 prediction proved heartbreakingly accurate. Darla recovered and Duffy didn't. Checking the puppies at least hourly, I discovered at one of those checks that Duffy didn't stir when I stroked him. He was gone.

Darla rallied and continued to improve until she went home in a few days. It is a disappointment to me that her owner failed to learn as much from Darla's struggle and Duffy's death as I did.

I think he returned with Darla one time, but he never asked me to spay her or perform her preventive care. I try to hope that he just found another vet more convenient to him, yet no one has ever called for her records or her medical history.

Some owners truly feel that their pets don't need a vet unless they get sick. They underestimate all we can do to keep pets healthy, saving the animals' suffering and their owners' money.

There is still a preposterous belief that veterinarians are out to gouge consumers at the expense of their pets. On the other hand, we all know owners who have pets only to use them, not to love them. I wonder which explains Darla's neglect: ignorance or greed?

It is tragic that these puppies suffered so, when a readily available vaccine could have prevented the disaster. At least Darla survived, and Duffy did not die in vain.

I am a more empathetic doctor because of this experience, and we at Applebrook gained confidence in our resourcefulness. I tell this story often to advocate prevention, and I truly appreciate my current isolation ward, which is no longer in my closet!

To this day, when I walk into my closet, my brain conjures The Odor of parvovirus and the picture of floppy ears and sad eyes giving me The Look. I rejoice when I think of Darla, but I just can't get Duffy out of that closet.

9. TicTac

Good things come in small packages, right? Consider TicTac. She is a Chihuahua, just over 4 pounds, tiny like the candy for which she's named, and every bit as sweet. She is affectionate, and she enchants everyone who gets to meet her.

She's a shoulder dog, with a distinct preference for the right shoulder. (If you put her on your left, she will squirm until she makes it over to the right.) She has a knack for making whoever is holding her feel like the center of the universe, which probably explains how she retains her supremacy.

TicTac's short biography is a pitiful litany of health problems. In the two short months since her adoption, I have treated her for three serious conditions.

Each breed of dog is at risk for its own list of diseases, and I have teased her owner that she should not have let TicTac read the

Chihuahua book because she seems to have begun working her way systematically through the list of her breed's illnesses. Happily for TicTac, fate landed her with Stacy, a dog's (and vet's) dream of an owner.

She is bubbly and fun, dedicated and loving. She is tuned in to her dogs and intelligent, with good judgment about when to seek help. I feel lucky that Stacy chose me to provide that help.

TicTac started with seizure disorder, which landed her at UT College of Veterinary Medicine for an MRI. That condition is well managed now with daily medication, and the seizure disorder does not interfere with her quality of life.

Like most small breed dogs, TicTac also suffers from periodontal disease. Stacy has made sure that her dental care is comprehensive and consistent, which is the only way to prevent what can be very severe tooth pain and adverse consequences for her general well-being.

When her mom noticed swelling in TicTac's abdomen, it turned out that this time TicTac had found herself a disease that wasn't on the

Chihuahua checklist. Since she had only recently been rescued, we all assumed that she was just gaining weight on her new regimen of security, nutrition, and love.

She was behaving normally and did not seem ill, but Stacy wanted to have her seen, to be safe rather than sorry. It turned out to be a very good call!

TicTac's body weight was increased by more than 10% due to a uterus so engorged with fluid that it might rupture at any moment. With no further warning, her entire abdomen could be flooded with infection.

Her situation then would become dire and her chance of survival would decrease dramatically. She needed to be spayed immediately. We asked our afternoon clients to reschedule their appointments, and they all agreed, to help save TicTac's life.

We took her straight into surgery in time to remove the uterus without complications, and TicTac made an uneventful recovery.

It was amazing how normally she had behaved while carrying that enormous diseased organ in her belly. She is a testament to resilience in the animal kingdom, as Stacy is a paragon of sensitivity among owners. A less attentive owner could have missed the changes in her dog, who was not even complaining a little bit.

Not every owner is willing to stick with a special needs dog. Not every owner is tuned in enough to notice subtle changes like TicTac's abdominal swelling.

TicTac and I are both fortunate to know Stacy. I hope and believe that when TicTac snuggles up on her mom's shoulder (the right, of course), she repays Stacy in triplicate for every moment of worry and all the burdens of treatment, past, present, and—no doubt, since the Chihuahua disease list is long, and she has only just begun—future.

10. I'm Scared, Yarn It!

Pedro is a gorgeous cat, long and lean, the quintessential Siamese. His dark extremities are the deepest velvet brown, the color of Hershey's Special Dark chocolate, a stark and beautiful contrast to his coat of butter cream.

I use food metaphors because comparing him to all things sweet makes such a perfectly ironic paradox for the Pedro I first knew. He was an angel at home, according to his owner, Holly, the perfect pet and companion, but we never got to see that.

When he came through the hospital door, he behaved as one possessed. Look at him and he erupted in a ferocious caterwaul. Touch him and he reenacted scenes from *The Exorcist*.

As a rational veterinary staff, we try to avoid treating dangerous animals. We were prepared to see Pedro, however, and to do our best for him at any time, because Holly was as lovable as Pedro was hateful.

She is a young and pretty blonde with a ready smile. She refers her friends and family to Applebrook, singing our praises. A registered nurse, she is always dressed rather casually out of uniform, though we noticed from the start that she rarely wore sweaters.

She is an educated and attentive consumer. She listens to our suggestions for Pedro's care and she asks germane questions. Holly is remorseful about the way her gorgeous cat behaves, and she worries about our safety.

Sedatives therefore have played a major role in Pedro's safe handling. (I had a professor once who liked to quote the DuPont motto: "Better living through chemistry." Pedro is the poster child for this slogan.)

He was a hissing, snarling, growling ball of fear and self-defense at my hospital. He wasn't evil; he was just very dangerous when he was afraid.

Fear and anxiety were Pedro's Achilles heel. Acute anxiety precipitated the madness we saw during treatment, and chronic anxiety had another manifestation.

Pedro was (and still is) Holly's closest confidante. Now she has other loves, both pets and people, to warm her heart, but when we met, it was Holly and Pedro against the world. The two of them shared a bond like mine with Merlin when he and I were facing vet school.

Pedro never did anything rude at home, except that he was such a mommy's boy, so bonded to Holly, that whenever she would leave him, anxiety would provoke him to **eat** her clothes, especially her sweaters.

After she had been gone a day or two, Pedro would ransack her closet or pounce on any other opportunity to chew the indigestible, removing clothing from hangers and upholstery from pillows. He would methodically unravel the yarn or fabric and swallow it inch by inch until he became desperately sick. He even required emergency gastrointestinal surgery.

I treated poor Pedro's beat-up intestinal tract way too often, to relieve the vomiting and gastritis he brought upon himself. He always recovered uneventfully and returned home with his grateful owner, only to resume his peculiar and dangerous dance with pica.

Why was he eating her sweaters? How could we stop him?

The unique challenge of veterinary medicine is that a troubled animal cannot tell you how it feels to be left alone, confused and frightened. He cannot explain his reasons for helping himself to Holly's clothing. My research on this type of problem revealed that Pedro is not alone.

Some experts believe that such behaviors are related to stress. The disordered behavior, in Pedro's case, pica, stimulates a comforting release of the hormone (oxytocin) that counteracts the adrenalin that makes him frantic. In other words, eating sweaters may be Pedro's equivalent of thumb sucking, a throwback to nursing as an infant.

Whether Pedro is neurotic or suffers a true biochemical abnormality in his brain is debatable. What may have started as neurosis could have led to brain changes, or vice versa.

Either way, Pedro suffered from a mental illness that included his over-the-top reaction to the stress of veterinary visits and his suicidal left-behind diet.

Holly and I discussed these findings. Because of her nursing expertise, she was interested in trying a mental health approach to relieving Pedro's self-destruction. First, we explored environmental modifications, hoping to isolate and identify anxiety triggers and remove potential hazards.

Unfortunately, separation was an anxiety trigger that simply could not be removed; Holly had to travel and couldn't take Pedro. And that clothes closet proved to be the most significant environmental hazard, but rendering it inaccessible drove Pedro even deeper into his particular madness.

Clearly, another strategy was called for, so we chose to try some off-label pharmaceutical therapy. We discovered a human anxiety medication that proved effective at a dosage calculated for cats.

(Felines are very sensitive to meds, especially human ones, and require very small amounts. Even then, they must be prescribed and supervised by a veterinarian.)

Sometimes cats are a challenge to medicate at home, but not Pedro. Whatever Holly does to him, he submits to without a struggle. He never resists her and he never, ever holds a grudge...against her.

He took this medication regularly for a while without incident. He even learned to take it hidden in a treat (a trick Merlin taught me), so a friend could medicate him when Holly was traveling. He survived her next absence with flying colors and without passing any colors!

Holly substituted other comfort items he could use to soothe himself without harming himself, and gradually he became accustomed to them. As his anxious behaviors stabilized, we weaned him from the daily medications.

Since Pedro's adrenaline levels came down long enough for him to experience the world differently and learn some new behaviors, he and Holly have managed his chronic anxiety without relying on meds. I have not treated Pedro for gastritis for a very long time.

I wish that I could say the medication also treated the acute anxiety Pedro suffered here at the hospital. It would be nice if we could cuddle him now and play with him. Since we still can't, I take my pleasure from knowing he is no longer so miserable that he has to eat indigestible fabrics. At least he does not have to confront the hospital phobia as often as he once did.

At his last visit here, I did manage to pet his head for just a moment for the first time ever. What really thrills me is that he no longer requires pharmacological treatment for stress or medical intervention for its disastrous consequences.

Yes, Pedro still enjoys less than complete mental health. He is so afraid of me that he cannot feel grateful. But we did improve his quality of life, and we did it without exorcism!

11. Desperate Housedogs

If a little old cat can be as fierce as Pedro was, it won't surprise you to know that, "It's not the size of the dog in the fight, but the size of the fight in the dog," is true. I see its many faces in my work.

Certain types of dogs live up to their breeding and to the average person's expectations. Big burly dogs with tough barks, like Rottweilers and Mastiffs, will usually step up to a challenge the way they look like they would. They walk the walk and talk the talk just as you might expect.

When you think of dog bites, you probably think of such dogs, the toughest looking, the ones you see in police movies. If you were ranking dogs from toughest and most likely to bite all the way to cutest and cuddliest, where would you start?

As a veterinarian, I just have to be calm and use common sense when dealing with potentially dangerous animals. The good news is that if a big dog is aggressive or unpredictable, he is likely to be strapping and healthy and win most of his fights; I won't see him very often.

Little dogs, the ones that raid kitchen trash or linger underfoot, see me more often—for pancreatitis, eating human medications, or broken bones. The cuddly little house dog knows and trusts people. Therefore, even if she is a bit accident prone, she is a wonderful and grateful patient, right? Not so fast!

A recent veterinary journal did a retrospective study of dog breeds that bite veterinarians. Would you believe that the #1 biter of veterinarians was the Chihuahua? It didn't surprise me.

Although I have many Chihuahua patients who would never dream of biting me or anyone else, other Chihuahuas have indeed wanted to bite me and had to be won over with bribery and their owners' help. Then there was Sweetie, strange and unreachable, impervious to bribes.

We all wore leather gloves to handle Sweetie, and we saw her so often that one of my assistants had ample opportunity to quantify her bites.

"Sweetie can bite me 17 times between the cage and the table" she marveled.

Why was Sweetie with us so often? I cannot tell you. I never got a confirmed diagnosis on any of her visits. If there was anything wrong with Sweetie besides her attitude, I suppose it might have had something to do with her mother's social arrangements.

Melissa was an attractive single female who obviously cared a great deal about Sweetie. It was really too bad that Sweetie was such a problem we couldn't adequately examine her. Nevertheless, Melissa faithfully brought her to us every Monday and Thursday around 4:00 in the afternoon.

Since my hospital is conveniently located close to home for Melissa, as it is for most of my clients—that's often what first brings them in—it didn't surprise me that whenever Melissa and Sweetie showed up, her neighbor Randy would appear too.

It only stood to reason that as he was driving past on the way home from work to the neighborhood, he would notice a familiar car in my parking lot, right? And he was a big, handsome guy, clearly designed for rescuing damsels in distress. Obviously, he stopped to help poor Melissa with her unruly little dog.

Although Randy the helpful neighbor drove a recognizable truck, with his employer's logo on the doors, surely there could be no cause for scandal when it so regularly parked beside Melissa's little white convertible. Everyone knew that Sweetie was a terrible trial. Who could question Randy's obliging presence at her visits to the veterinary hospital? Anyway, Randy had a dog of his own, didn't he?

The first time they came, Melissa claimed Sweetie had been urinating inappropriately for a few days. We were still in the exam room when Randy arrived and joined us. Terri, my technician, and I assumed he was Sweetie's dad, so we included him in the history taking to attempt to define the problem.

At the time, I thought nothing of his involvement because I did not know that he was only a neighbor. Looking back, I realized that, for a neighbor, he knew a lot about Sweetie's life style, personality, and behavior.

Sweetie showed attitude that day, forever putting us on our mettle against her hatred of all handling. Here's what I mean.

Usually we take a urine sample by following the patient around the yard with a ladle. Sweetie's refusal to be approached meant we performed her urinalysis using specimens collected from the floor.

I did not find abnormalities in her urine, but such findings are not unusual. We discussed medical and behavioral causes of inappropriate urination and sent her and her chaperones on their way.

At the next visit, Sweetie had fallen off an embankment at a nearby construction site, causing Melissa visible distress. I didn't understand how the morbidly obese Sweetie had managed to walk down the street to a construction site, but Melissa was obviously in a heightened state of tension.

We proceeded to the exam room and began gloving up for the physical exam. It was very difficult to judge whether the fall had left Sweetie sore or stiff because she reacted equally violently no matter where or how I touched her.

Before much time had passed, Randy was escorted into the room. This time, he introduced himself as Melissa and Sweetie's neighbor. He explained that he had seen their car as he drove by on his way home. Knowing what a problem Sweetie could be, he had felt he should stop to see if we or Melissa needed help. We didn't.

We had to sedate Sweetie to examine and radiograph her thoroughly, and I was relieved to find no abnormalities. During the sedation and radiology, the owner and her hovering companion remained in the exam room alone talking in hushed whispers.

Eventually my entire staff and I began to notice an evolving pattern of unnecessary visits by Sweetie, attended by Randy, who never touched the dog or assisted Melissa in any visible way. Such curious patterns of events quicken the imagination of a veterinary staff, and my staff began to develop an interesting explanation. They hypothesized that...

The pair was using our hospital as a clandestine meeting place.

(No!)

Perhaps they were madly in love, destined to be together but facing insurmountable obstacles.

(What could those be?)

Had Randy been wearing a wedding ring?

(Hadn't he?)

Could it be that both or one was married, but not to each other?

(Gasp!)

Sensationalism makes headlines and romantic sensationalism is the best kind.

(Sigh.)

Terri and the other assistants had fun embellishing theories and debating details. I, of course, was above such trivial matters.

(Blush.)

Sweetie reportedly suffered many small traumas over the next several weeks. Presumably, none of them was serious. (Remember, we could not examine or diagnose her without anesthesia, which I was unwilling to use for problems that increasingly looked factitious.) Each time Melissa brought her in,

Randy would join her very soon, serving no useful purpose to Sweetie or us.

We therefore came to believe that the original theory must be correct: we were playing host to a couple of star-crossed lovers. Nevertheless, pitiable as it must certainly be to have such an accident-prone dog (or lurid imagination), even simple neighborly support might conceivably be quite welcome.

Unfortunately, Randy turned out to be one of those big dogs without much fight. After the day his wife showed up, we never again had the pleasure of his company.

On that last Thursday afternoon, Mrs. Randy brought the family dog for a routine visit. We had never seen her or her dog before, but we were glad they came, and we had sent for her previous vet's records, which indicated that her pet was not quite due for his yearly physical examination.

No one asked her how she came to choose Applebrook Animal Hospital. Naturally, since she lived in our neighborhood, she would choose us, wouldn't she. The only question was, "Why now?"

Her dog was not difficult to handle, but the appointment occurred just before Sweetie usually made her appearance, and I somehow expected chivalrous Randy to be at his own dog's examination.

He didn't make it, and his wife wryly noted his absence. Her dog got a clean bill of health, and she was leaving the building just as Randy came through the door on the heels of Sweetie and Melissa.

He turned right around and left with his wife, who never brought her pet back to Applebrook. Apparently, one visit to us was all it took. I wonder how we offended her.

We never saw Sweetie again either. It seems unlikely that so susceptible an animal would abruptly have stopped venturing onto construction sites and tumbling off couches. Perhaps this noble little dog was embarrassed that we had seen how accident-prone she tended to be.

Yes, that must be the explanation. After all, if she wasn't afraid to take us on, she couldn't be afraid of Mrs. Randy's raised eyebrow.

Could she?

12. Manning Up

Among the dedicated pet owners I see every day, Matt holds the record. He and his dog, Manning, demonstrated almost unimaginable devotion, the like of which one encounters with awe. What a couple of men they were!

Manning was a spotted Dalmatian who was adopted at a young age, but I didn't see him until he was an adult. He had been hit by a car when he was 13 months old, and by the time I was privileged to become part of his care 7 years later, he was starting to experience stiffness and joint pain.

You could see some change in his musculature from not being able to use himself as well as he might have, but Manning was one happy dog. The guy seemed to smile at you each time he saw you.

His dad did not like to see the deterioration from his joint pain, so we started looking for treatments that might address it. I knew that

Manning's old hip injury was probably to blame for at least part of his pain because old injuries are typical sites for the chronic bone and joint inflammation known to dogs and people as osteoarthritis.

This disease becomes common with age, so I suggested that we radiograph Manning's hips, spine, and knees in order to grade his disease and guide treatment. Matt agreed, and off to radiology we went.

To my consternation, the disease process proved to be much more advanced than Manning was showing behaviorally. The hip that had been repaired after his run-in with the car was affected, as I had thought, but even more severe lesions appeared along his spine. This suggested that besides osteoarthritis, Manning was suffering from intervertebral disc disease.

Radiographs are an excellent means to check for fractures and changes in bone because they so clearly show bony lesions and defects. These were wretchedly plain in Manning's x-rays: I could see a painful process called spondylosis.

The spine is made up of bones (vertebrae) that look almost like train cars lined up to support and encase the spinal cord, the bundle of nerves that transmits between brain and limbs the signals for pain and instructions for movement. Instability in the spine leads to inflammation and pain, and the body responds by laying down extra bone.

That is spondylosis.

It's as if the body constructs a sort of bridge to fuse the joint space between vertebrae, to correct the instability. These bridges were present on almost every joint space along Manning's spine. He was at risk of disc herniation and paralysis.

Intervertebral disc disease can be a slow and insidious process; sometimes it seems like all you can do is wait to see how it progresses, which feels like waiting for the axe to fall.

When I showed Manning's images to his dad and explained what they meant, Matt was determined to be more proactive. He loved Manning too much to resign himself to passive waiting and palliative care. He wanted to return the devotion that he had always received from his remarkable pet.

He bowed his head for a moment, and then asked, "What now?"

He was not all right with just hoping that Manning might not become paralyzed. It might be too late by then, and anyway, he wanted to tackle Manning's pain proactively.

I referred him and Manning to a specialist to plan their next steps.

As the dog continued to age, his rear quarters did become paralyzed, but Matt was not discouraged. He consulted more specialists, bought special equipment (doggie wheels), kept every physical therapy appointment, and brought his dog to me for regular monitoring.

While Manning was lying on my treatment table, one of my assistants would feed him treats bite by bite as long as he would eat them or until the treatment was finished. His appetite usually outlasted the treatment, and he showed himself no worse for all the wear.

A paralyzed pet has very special needs and requires an overwhelming amount of exquisitely careful TLC. While he provided all that care, Matt's heart broke for Manning, but Manning's heart continued always full of joy and love. He lay still so we could treat whatever new challenge had appeared, from pressure sores to infections, and he was grateful for every bit of attention (and treats).

Matt was the only one who could lift the Dalmatian to situate him in his wheelchair, and it grew more and more exhausting for him to give Manning the 24/7 attention he required. But it was important to him that Manning survive as long as he had that gleam in his eye, so he mustered the stamina from some limitless source of resolve.

He built ramps all over their house so Manning could navigate with his wheels, but the fact remained that only Matt was strong enough to lift Manning. Sam, Matt's lovely petite wife, was just not strong enough to manage the dog even if she didn't already have her hands full with their toddler.

Since Matt's job required travel, he decided that Manning must accompany him so that Sam was never left helpless alone with

Manning. No longer could Matt fly to his business destinations.

He had to drive so that Manning could ride along. He had to study weather forecasts to plan his travel for dates that would allow Manning to wait in the car only in temperate weather. He had to pack not only his own bag but also the enormous amount of paraphernalia that a paralyzed dog requires.

Manning was not able to urinate on his own; Matt had to use massage to help him evacuate his bladder. Matt and Sam learned some physical therapy exercises to help Manning at home. They fed him and cleaned up after him, helped him with his every need, even waking up in the middle of the night to turn him, attempting to avoid bedsores.

Matt's dedication to his canine friend was awe-inspiring and Sam's dedication to Matt is equally breathtaking. Sleepless nights and caregiver's fatigue catch up with all of us but they held on. As hard as it is to sacrifice yourself daily for someone you love, it is even harder to sacrifice your heart finally when it's time to let go.

The day had to come when Manning's fire could burn no more. Everyone on my staff from Chuck, our practice manager, to Julie, my vet assistant, rallied to mourn his passing. Manning's families from Applebrook and home gathered around him on the grass beneath a tree in the hospital yard.

We held each other and we held Manning as he ate the treats we fed him for the last time. The world seemed to pause there under that tree with time standing still. We were grateful for a merciful passing for Manning, who must have felt all our love as he crossed over Rainbow Bridge, leaving the legacy of his and Matt's boundless gallantry.

13. Soldier's Creed

Otis was a soldier. A lean, muscular Boxer dog with an expressive face and stoic disposition, he would give his life for his friends without a second thought. He exuded that kind of intelligent, watchful calm that filled a room.

You felt safe with Otis beside you; you knew he had your back. He was a guardian. He would never stray from duty and he would never accept defeat. You embraced these traits in Otis...most of the time.

After a fight, Otis came to me one day with savage wounds that were not what we expect from ordinary neighborhood canine disputes. No one had seen the contretemps, so we will never know for sure what really happened. It must have been some fight, though. The result, which we could see, was fearsome.

The wounds were large, deep, and jagged. Obviously, some threat to Otis's home had provoked his defense of it. Since those terrible injuries were on his face, neck, and shoulder, there could be no doubt that he had stood to face the threat and did not retreat.

An old joke quips, "You should have seen the other guy!" The other party to this dispute, who was nowhere to be found, must have been a mess for sure. Otis had to have been the undisputed victor, and with characteristic courage and stamina, he faced the immediate price and the long-term costs.

He didn't whimper about the bite wounds, which were accompanied by tissue trauma and bruising, always painful and slow to resolve. He barely limped.

He held himself perfectly still as I assessed his injuries, while Julie stroked him and soothingly whispered sweet nothings. He seemed to know that **we** were not the cause of his misery, keeping his trusting gaze upon me as he listened to Julie.

He appeared stressed but stable, so we began preparations for wound care. (Since the lacerations were so extensive, we used anesthesia to immobilize him and spare him pain during the long process.)

The gash on his shoulder was especially cavernous, requiring surgical repair. Then, because bite wounds are always contaminated, we placed a drain to prevent formation of a closed abscess.

The area looked much less scary by the time we finished and roused Otis, but I knew he was facing an uncomfortable week, to say the least. I did all I could to ease his discomfort with medication, but he had other fights ahead of him whenever the pain struck back in force.

His owner soon reported that Otis was himself again. His rapid recovery was amazing in the face of all that damage: Otis simply did not surrender.

True to his uncompromising nature, once he began to feel better Otis decided that he could dispense with the nuisance of the drain, and he set to work to lose it. The Battle of the Drain required countless attacks, gritted teeth, and body contortions that can scarcely be imagined, as he had to work around a cone collar designed to *keep* him from the drain.

Otis worried that drain until he first removed the sutures that were intended to hold it securely to his skin, and then he removed the drain itself. Triumphant at last... Oh, wait, there's more... He discovered and set out to remove the very sutures that held the wound itself closed.

Again, Otis was resolute. He opened the top third of his wound, exposing the damaged tissue inside. The macabre laceration had to be surgically cleaned up and closed again, followed by a second round of antibiotics.

Finally, we were able to outsmart that boy so he could heal, but it wasn't easy. We used stainless steel staples instead of sutures. (I hate to think of the consequences if he had reached those!) Furthermore, this time we devised a collar and bandage combination that did work to keep him away from the closures until I was ready to remove them.

Otis perfectly modeled not good sense, perhaps, but the epitome of persistence in the face of the enemy. If he could surmount barriers as challenging as that collar... If he would accept serious injuries but never forfeit the contest... If he could do this to himself in order to defeat an intruder like that drain, which didn't move or speak... Can you imagine what he would do to protect his home and family?

No wonder he came to me with such wounds. With bravery and stoicism, he had defended his territory and his home, perhaps from wild animals, regardless of pain and injury. He withstood surgical repairs and infections, taking them in his inexorable stride. We should all be so tough.

Otis lived to be nearly 12 years old, exceeding the typical Boxer life span by a good two years—and they were very good years. The old soldier always exhibited that undaunted good cheer and fortitude.

14. Simple Fideles

My 16-year-old step-dog had passed away. It was a terrible loss: my husband had loved him before he loved me, and Seven, our middle-aged Doberman missed him dreadfully. If our family was to be whole again, we were going to have to find another rescue dog.

Seven did not have a dominant personality and she wasn't getting any younger. We needed our new dog to be a docile companion to her while we were away all day and an equable playmate for baby Will as he grew up.

We decided on a large breed dog. We like big dogs, of course, but we had ulterior motives. Larger dogs are sometimes harder to place than smaller dogs are, and I hoped we would be providing a necessary service. Since big dogs are less in demand, I also assumed that we might complete our family that much sooner. Boy, was I wrong!

When I contacted large-dog rescue groups, specifically for giants like Great Danes, I was shocked to discover that many of them rejected me instantly. I'm quite a charming person, with experience as a pet owner, good credit, nice family, and no criminal record. What on earth didn't they like about me?

I even made sure they knew that I was a qualified veterinarian! Still, they rejected me.

I persisted until one screener finally explained that I was not a good candidate because of **"The Child."** Her chilly words still resound in my memory:

"Great Danes and children are a very poor mix."

Well... Will was here to stay, so I gritted my teeth, thanked her coolly, and hung up.

I did not give up, of course, and in a city about 100 miles away, I found a rescue organization that sponsored giant and large breed dogs and liked me. They were thrilled that they had hooked a vet who was looking for a big dog.

I asked very pointedly, "Do you have a dog that <u>needs</u> to belong to a veterinarian?" explaining that I know certain dogs require care that not everyone can provide or is willing to give, and emphasizing that I wanted to provide a home for a dog who might not have any other available choices.

The screener replied, "Oh, yes, ma'am!" and went on to describe an 8-month-old Great Dane named Dora, who had been seized from a very bad environment. Dora had had a broken leg that had never been set correctly and her very severe skin condition had defied all treatments to date.

She had been living in foster care with a veterinary technician who took her to work frequently, but despite the care she received there, Dora's black coat was so moth-eaten that she appeared from a distance to have spots like the harlequin color for her breed. She had received so many different medications at so many different dosages that she had suffered adverse side effects.

The rescue group emailed photos, faxed medical records, and shared enchanting stories of Dora's gentle personality. I looked at the photos of moth-eaten hair, perused the medical history, and enjoyed the stories.

To the very heart of me, I knew that Dora was the dog for us. I felt confident that I could treat her skin condition and manage the residual lameness from her old injuries.

When I called back and explained that we wanted Dora, I finally screwed up my courage and mentioned that we had a baby.

The woman who spoke to me laughed excitedly and exclaimed, "How wonderful! When can we bring Dora to you?" confirming my belief in the dog's golden temperament.

She went on to explain that Dora's failure to respond to treatment had kept her from finding a loving home, which had begun to jeopardize her existence. Their budget for treatment had been stretched as far as it could reach to meet Dora's needs, and her adoption crisis was becoming urgent. Unquestionably, this was our dog.

She was the breed we wanted, she needed **us**, she needed us *now*, and the rescue connection was congenial. They were willing to drive her 100 miles to place her in a home where she would get what she needed, so much devotion had she inspired. I knew absolutely that we were right for each other.

And so it proved to be. Dora is 8 years old this year and still an indispensable part of our family. She stayed by Seven's side all through her life, keeping her playful and entertained to the end of her days.

Now Dora is our senior pet, and she has shepherded foster dogs and befriended cats with her stalwart company. She is serenely tolerant of the ever-changing menagerie that fills the home of a vet.

Her legs tremble sometimes from the side effects of that long ago medication error that probably caused some mild nerve damage, but her black coat has been glossy and shiny since a few months after she got to our house.

She has a little bit of a limp from the crooked-healing front leg that resulted from her early injury, and she suffers some osteoarthritis that comes with the territory for a big dog that is aging, but Dora still runs and plays and barks.

She has a terrific life and we love her. She is without a doubt the sweetest and most loyal dog ever born, and she has the kindest spirit. She comes when you call her and she will stay by your side as long as you are touching her.

Dora and Will have grown up together. She is his brave warhorse charger, carrying his wooden sword and shield in a pack on her back. They lie in sunbeams with his head on her midsection. When Will is out of sight and Dora hears his voice, she barks insistently until he shows himself. She watches after him and I know that she would lay down her life for him.

Great Danes and children are a poor mix? Nonsense. She is our boy's best friend, playmate, and guardian, and she asks nothing in return. She is simply faithful.

Epilogue

Kismet

I was born to be a veterinarian. I knew it as a child. The kittens I let "out of the bag" as a new vet and Merlin with his endless challenges confirmed it. As I hope the foregoing tales convey, I have felt it every day in practice. If any doubt remained, the universe offered final proof during Memorial Day weekend in 1999.

My journey began on horseback when I was five, though I later discovered that I was not meant for a career in large animal medicine. Naturally, given Mother Nature's sense of humor, it is on horseback that this final story begins, just as Applebrook Animal Hospital is about to celebrate its first anniversary.

In need of recreation and a change of scenery, I strap on my pager and head to the mountains for a rare outing on horseback with my best friend, Shannon, her husband,

and several novice riders from our boarding stable. My friends and I are the only experienced riders on the trail, and I am the only one wearing a helmet.

(Since my college days when my roommate and I rode Hunter/Jumper, I have always worn a helmet. It is standard riding attire for jumping, and I am always conscientious about protective gear.) I note that none of the novices is appropriately attired. I even whisper to my friends that I hope no one gets stepped on with nothing but tennis shoes between their toes and the horse's hoof. Do I somehow know that trouble is coming?

We head off up the side of the mountain. The sunny spring is beautiful and serene. Winding trails overlook leaf-strewn valleys, and the air is alive with the sounds of birds. I can feel myself relaxing.

Since my own show horse is not calm enough for trail riding, I have borrowed a horse for this ride. She is a lovely dark bay Quarter Horse, and I like her well enough that I might consider buying her as my trail mount. Today I am putting her through her paces.

As I work with the horse, trying to see how responsive she is, I am giving her commands, asking her to turn her head and break at the poll. These are easy tasks, and she is doing very well until a sapling hangs up under her breast collar.

She's broad through the chest, as Quarter Horses ought to be, and I have no view of what's happening up front. Not knowing why she has paused in sudden disregard of my commands, I ask her again to give me her head and back up. Reluctantly, she obeys. She bows her head and puts all her considerable strength into backing.

As her powerful hindquarters exert steady force, the breast collar, which has been held by the sapling, abruptly snaps in two. The force released sends the saddle—and me—right over my mount's rump, and my lights go out. I land on my head, unconscious...

Shannon rushed to help me, saw that my pupils were different sizes, and knew that my condition was critical. Someone raced to the nearest house and called 911. The Life Force helicopter responded, but we were so far from a road or any other potential landing space that the crew had to carry me quite some distance on a stretcher.

I had no identification with me; my family was called on the basis of information provided by my friends. My mother says that when she arrived, she couldn't find out whether I was dead or alive.

[She remembers that in the frenzy of activity and fear, someone (she never knew who) gave her a small, yellow, sealed envelope containing my jewelry. She wasn't reassured when she saw that the envelope was labeled "Jane Doe."]

I was unconscious during all of this, spared the anxiety and dread of those around me. How terrible it must have been for them; how I regret that they had to endure it.

I had suffered head trauma with a broken jaw and a broken collarbone. During surgery to repair my jaw I suffered some anesthetic complications and was kept in a medically induced coma for a while.

My husband never left me. When others tried to persuade him to go home and rest, he steadfastly refused; he would not leave. And then—poor Shane—when I finally awoke, I didn't even recognize him.

My short-term memory was impaired. I could not remember from one moment to the next who the people were that surrounded me. Due to either the brain injury or damage to my middle ear, I couldn't even walk.

Everyone kept asking me sympathetically what I thought and how I was feeling. Well, I *thought* I was going to be completely all right, and I was *feeling* altogether tranquil. I hated to disappoint them, but in truth, I felt a sense of peace and calm that I have never forgotten.

I knew I was OK. I was confident that I could cope with whatever came, and I was not afraid. The early serenity of that ultimately disastrous spring day seemed to have entered my soul.

Everyone else feared that I would never recover, never walk, never again be me. My father admits that he was afraid I would not remember how to be a veterinarian. He need not have worried.

In the midst of all that, when I could not tell the time of day or even the date, I always remembered my professional training. Shane has told me that in one breath, I'd ask who he was and in the next, I'd speak knowledgeably about drugs named in my medical chart.

With physical therapy, I began to regain my ability to walk. With occupational therapy, I made sure I was able to perform surgery and other work-related physical tasks.

I started to regain my memory. Today I can remember most of the ordeal (at least the part when I was conscious) up to about 5 minutes before I crash-landed and then picking up the thread again in the hospital's step-down unit. I have no very clear recollection of my time in the ICU, which I understand is probably a good thing.

I do remember well my time at the rehabilitation center as my drive to be me again grew stronger. I was confined to a wheelchair then, dependent on my family and caregivers for everything. I could scarcely go to the bathroom on my own.

This helplessness was daunting to my obstinately independent spirit. I wanted to "get the show on the road," and my belief that

I would recover was unflagging. A naturally impatient person, I found the demands of incapacity humbling, and grew stronger.

Remembering my early days in vet school, I struggled to suture "wounded" sponges to show my therapist that I was capable of stitching. To prove that I could calculate drug doses, administer injections, and perform other rudimentary medical tasks, I let her test me as if I were a student again.

The veterinary part was easy, though.

The walking and remembering parts proved more difficult. Traumatic brain injury (TBI) has physical consequences you can understand only by experience. When I was finally released, I was in a wheelchair, and looking at the world from there forever enriched my empathy for those who cope with disability.

Those kind and patient therapists and nurses who looked after me and taught me will remain forever in my heart. I strive to be like them, intervening to alter injury and illness as much as I can for the better, hoping I can be as gracious to my patients as they were to me.

Returning to work in my own hospital after six difficult weeks, I brought the residual effects of TBI an ever stronger conviction that I am doing what I was meant to do. For this I survived a serious equestrian accident and returned from TBI with full retention of my veterinary skills and practice knowledge.

The pearls of wisdom I have earned through this confirm the rest of my life experience: we are in this together.

I would not be alive without my friends who raced to get help for me.

I would not be whole without my family who lovingly supported me. I owe the professional healthcare providers who skillfully assisted and taught me.

I could not do my job, which thrills and amuses me, without staff like Julie and Chuck (and many others along the way), who read my mind and anticipate my needs.

I would not be who I am without the clients who have trusted me and the animals that have inspired me.

I love you all.

Kathryn Primm, DVM

About the Author

Kathryn Primm, DVM really does reside in Tennessee. She spends her days practicing at Applebrook Animal Hospital and collecting more stories. *Tennessee Tails: Pets and Their People* is her first book.

If you would like to be notified when her next title becomes available, visit her website at www.drprimm.com and click on the envelope. Your email address will never be shared or sold, and you can unsubscribe at any time.

Dr. Primm's appearance schedule is also posted on the web site. She loves to meet readers and to talk about animals and communication, her two passions. She has a presence on Facebook (Kathryn Primm dvm), Google+, and Twitter (DrKathrynPrimm).

If you like these "tails", please consider leaving a review on Amazon. Even brief feedback is valuable; it could influence the next collection!

Made in the USA
San Bernardino, CA
29 October 2015